THE

FRIENDSHIP

ADVANTAGE

7 Keys to Building Relationships
that Transform Corporate Culture
and Drive Productivity

Mo Fathelbab

Trusted by more than 20,000 CEOs,
author of
*Forum: The Secret Advantage of
Successful Leaders*

Dedicated to my mom, dad and my late maternal grandparents and my loving extended family. You did well – and good at the same time!

Thank You

Thank you to all those who have contributed to this book. I'm grateful to each and every one of you. Elizabeth Trigg, who has been by my side for more than 10 years has been invaluable all along and has provided much support with launching this book, -- thank you! Thank you to my editor Rachael Garrity, who understands me and my work and provides years of experience from which I've benefited greatly. Thank you to Emmet Rosenfeld for further editorial guidance. Thank you to Devin Hurley Zarus for help with artwork and design.

A special thanks to Chris Johnson, CEO of Hollister Construction Services, for being a dear friend, a dream client and for giving me access to all his staff for this project. Thank you Greg Richards and Jeff Marowits of Keystone Strategy for their support both in trusting me with their most precious meetings and for their contribution to this book. Thank you Ashton Newhall, co-founder and managing partner of Greenspring Associates for the opportunity to work with him and his team. Thank you Lee Wang, COO of WeddingWIRE, for his support, friendship and the opportunity to work with his teams. Thank you to Matt Fleissig, president of Pathstone Federal Street, It is always a pleasure working with Matt and your team. Thank you to Jarl Mohn, Jennifer Lehman-Weng and Neil Balter for their friendship and support. Neil, you have been a role model and one of my true heroes in the world. You continue to amaze me with your courage, trans-parency, morals and how you truly treat everyone with love and respect even in the toughest of times.

Thank you Nancy Evans, former president of Doubleday for her powerful insights and invaluable input. Thank you Katrina VanHuss, CEO of Turnkey for her time, energy, support and thoughtful comments along the way.

No thank you would be complete without my eternal gratitude to Verne Harnish, founder and CEO of Gazelles International. Verne has impacted thousands of people both through his current organization and through founding Entrepreneurs' Organization. He has certainly changed my life for the better. Thank you!

Thank you to my executive coach, Helene Finizio, who has helped me and inspired me in many ways including the extra nudge to write this book.

Thank you to Sally Hurley, my life partner and to our son Eli for their love, support and for enduring my many travels. Sally is an amazing entrepreneur in her own right, the founder and CEO of VIPDesk Connect and her impact is certainly reflected in this book. My love to both of you.

Table of Contents

Disclaimer: Any scenes presented in this book are informed by Mo's experience with thousands of executives over the course of decades as a corporate trainer, but are entirely fictional and for illustrative purposes only. Mo maintains the highest standards of professionalism in tailoring his work to each client's needs, always honoring a strict confidentiality agreement.

Introduction

Karl is a 45-year old marketing executive for a mid-sized capital management firm based on the west coast. An exemplary performer for years, Karl has climbed steadily in the company, even garnering regional recognition for innovative efforts in the public-private sphere.

Lately, however, Karl's output has inexplicably plateaued. No huge fumbles, but little things: he missed targets in two consecutive quarters; team members were surprised when he showed up under-prepared for weekly meetings, something the "old Karl" would never do.

A managing partner calls Karl in to his office and is surprised when, after a few minutes of small talk, Karl breaks down.

"My wife has Stage 4 ovarian cancer," Karl reveals, fighting back tears. "She beat it eight years ago and we thought we were free and clear. But now it's back." The partner is stunned, finally able to manage a few words of condolence before the meeting winds down.

Karl's story is one we can probably all relate to at some level. Maybe, like him, we've experienced a family crisis that affects our work. Or, like his manager, we've been blindsided when projections are off or employee performance declines.

Certainly, the potential costs with a situation like this are clear: lower productivity in the short term; a vacuum in mid-level leadership; perhaps even the loss of a valued employee. Beyond these, there may be less tangible but equally significant impacts on company morale and corporate culture.

What happens next with Karl's story is what separates average companies from great ones. And it boils down to a simple question: does Karl work with friends?

If the answer is no— as it well might be, in a typical corporation-—the outcome is something along the lines of what is described above.

But if the answer to this question is yes, suddenly what seemed like an unfortunate but unpreventable tragedy turns into something completely different. Perhaps even something remarkable: an opportunity for growth, support and, ultimately, renewal.

Picture this: as Karl's wife begins to experience troubling fatigue and the early signs of a relapse, Karl confides in a good friend at work, a colleague in the marketing department. As her symptoms progress, rather than stuffing his problems and ignoring work, Karl finds a supportive network of colleagues, and even of other survivors who have experienced something similar to what he and his wife are going through.

As Karl's wife's health declines, Karl's managers are aware of his needs and find ways to lessen his load, recognizing that the emotional and physical toll of his wife's illness will inevitably affect Karl's productivity for a period of time.

As a gesture of solidarity and support, the firm joins a national cancer awareness campaign, fielding a team to participate in a walkathon and raising funds. Over 50 percent of Karl's co-workers contribute, and, as his wife slowly recovers, Karl has the life-affirming experience of joining his friends, with his wife at his side, in presenting a sizeable check to the charitable organization.

Eventually, Karl's wife beats the odds, and in turn, he returns to his old form. And then some. His experience of profound support—of friendship at work—has forged an indelible bond with his company. Both Karl and his co-workers, are affected. There is a general if unspoken awareness that in this place, people have value. They've got your back here, and in turn, a corporate culture is nourished that not only retains the best, but grows them to be better yet.

Does the better version of Karl's story sound far-fetched? Sadly, many might think so. But this doesn't have to be the case, for any business, small or large.

Smart leaders know that their number one asset is people. Through the application of a few simple principles which I share in this book, corporations can truly become places that nurture their employees, resulting in a culture that has a direct impact on not just their lives, but the bottom line.

So why listen to me? Allow me to share my story. As a kid, I struggled with self-esteem and finding my place socially. I often felt that I didn't fit in or I was less popular than I'd hoped. Sure, I always had friends but that didn't change my feelings. There were times I felt left out, and that flat out sucked and hurt.

I got to a low point when I went to bed crying, feeling sad and rejected. While that experience was very painful at the time, I'm eternally grateful for it. It gave me the fuel to light a fire and change my world in profound ways. I became obsessed with what it takes to become popular, to make lots of real friends and most of all to never feel this way again.

My personal pursuit became a 30+ year career in which my real focus (regardless of the stated purpose of the job or business) has been to use my knowledge to help thousands of people. Along the way I believe I've figured out what it takes to build real relationships.

Over the last five years, my work has shifted from 90 percent roundtables and CEO peer groups and 10 percent corporate to 60/40 respectively. I believe this is because there's a shift in focus on the importance of humanizing corporate culture.

Part of that shift is founded in the conscious capitalism movement, through which companies see their people as the real asset and not as a tool to achieving the company's goals. Emotional Intelligence is in the forefront, overshadowing IQ, and getting along at work is the bare minimum. Employees have many more

7

options, with record low unemployment rates and a globalized teleworking industry. The sweatshop model has been replaced by quality of life. Part of all that is the fact that people need to go to work and have relationships and connections. It's not enough to show up, do your job and collect a paycheck.

The suggestions in this book are not for everyone. I hope you'll look at each relationship in your life more critically through these seven keys and simply ask yourself: "Is any one of these keys a good way to unlock the potential of THIS relationship?"

You are the one to ultimately decide, and once you do decide, you are the one to make a change. In this book, you'll find the tools to help you move forward. It is my sincerest hope that after reading the book, you'll find greater joy and less pain in the important relationships in your life. Yes, the primary focus is on relationships in a work environment, but once you see the power, I'm guessing you'll want to examine all of your relationships.

One important thought that is critical as you embark upon this journey: It's easy to say, "I cannot change someone else," and based on that argument choose to take no responsibility.

In relationships, as in the law of physics, for every action, there's an equal and opposite reaction. There was a time when I didn't speak to my father for 10 years. As a young college student, I thought I knew everything, and I blamed him 100 percent for the state of our relationship. As I matured, I became convinced that I was 50 percent responsible and he held the other 50 percent. That seems very logical, but it didn't move the needle.

What finally did move the needle is when I decided to take 100 percent responsibility for the outcome. That doesn't mean I blamed myself for the past. Instead, I chose to take 100 percent responsibility for my future actions. That was the turning point that enabled me to rekindle a relationship that had been dead. I'm grateful to have had this insight. And, no, it wasn't easy to come by.

Now, I'm grateful that I have the chance to share what I've learned with you. I truly believe that these seven keys can unlock the power of friendship in your corporate culture in ways that are transformative.

Chapter

The Seven Keys to Real Relationships

. . . Just 30 percent of employees have a best friend at work. Those who do are seven times as likely to be engaged in their jobs, are better at engaging customers, produce higher quality work, have higher well-being, and are less likely to get injured on the job. In sharp contrast, those without a best friend in the workplace have *just a 1 in 12 chance of being engaged.*

- from *Wellbeing: The Five Essential Elements* by Tom Rath and Jim Harter, Ph.D.

The Seven Keys to Friendship:

Judgment-Free

Mischievous Fun

Vulnerability

Kind Truth

Reliability

Generosity

Shared Purpose.

I can't begin to tell you which is most critical or even the order in which they should fall. I can tell you that the order is different for everyone and that at least one of these keys will prove to be very difficult for you or those with whom you want to develop real relationships.

Overcoming this difficulty takes courage. It takes courage to be vulnerable, it takes courage to tell the truth, it takes courage to say "No" in order to keep your commitment, it takes courage to take on a shared purpose that may be out of your comfort zone, it takes courage to be generous when you don't have much to give and, yes, it takes courage to do something mischievous. It takes way more than courage to not judge someone, because judging is a natural default for so many of us.

This book is designed to simplify each of these concepts, so that you can understand the impact of each of the keys and easily apply whatever key you choose, if you have the courage!

Building Real Relationships

Building real relationships is a valuable life skill that can be learned by anyone and applied in all phases of life—personal and professional. Again, you have to choose how much you want to put into practice and with whom. You also get to choose with whom you are "all in."

You may be surprised to hear that building real relationships is important for your professional life, but I can tell you that it is critical to your success and the success of your company.

Friends at Work Add Value, Research Shows

It's no secret that to advance in the workplace, being competent is just the beginning. If you are competent and you have the skills to build real relationships, you'll be far more successful.

According to a Gallup research study of more than 80,000 managers, employees who report having a best friend at work were:

- ❖ 43 percent more likely to report having received praise or recognition for their work in the last seven days.

- ❖ 37 percent more likely to report that someone at work encourages their development.

- ❖ 35 percent more likely to report coworker commitment to quality.

- ❖ 28 percent more likely to report that in the last six months, someone at work has talked to them about their progress.

- ❖ 27 percent more likely to report that the mission of their company makes them feel their job is important.

- ❖ 27 percent more likely to report that their opinions seem to count at work.

- ❖ 21 percent more likely to report that at work, they have the opportunity to do what they do best every day.

Fostering Loyalty, Trust and Resilience

While companies often pay significant attention to loyalty toward the organization, the best employers recognize that loyalty toward one another also exists among employees.

All employees have "leaving moments" when they examine whether to leave or stay at an organization. The best managers in the world observe that the quality and depth of employees' relationships is a critical component of employee loyalty.

Equally important is the issue of trust between coworkers. When members of a work group feel strong engagement, they believe their coworkers will help them during times of stress and challenge.

In this day of rapid-fire change, reorganization, mergers and acquisitions, having best friends at work may be the true key to effective change integration and adaptation.

When compared to those who don't, employees who have best friends at work identify significantly higher levels of healthy stress management, even though they experience the same levels of stress.

Linkedin's Relationships @ Work study revealed that 46 percent of professionals worldwide believe that work friends are important to their overall happiness.

The survey was conducted by O.C. Tanner, a global employee recognition company based in Salt Lake City, Utah. The firm's clients include PepsiCo and The Home Depot. Here's a sampling of the key findings:

- ❖ 75 percent of employees who have a best friend at work say they feel they're able to take anything on, compared to 58 percent of those who don't have a best friend at work.

- ❖ 72 percent of employees who have a best friend at work are satisfied with their jobs, compared to 54 percent of those who don't have a best friend at work.

❖ Millennials (those born at any time between 1981 and 1997) top older generations when it comes to having a best friend at work. And the likelihood of having this type of connection goes down as age increases.

Engagement Improves Productivity

According to the *Harvard Business Review* people who have a "best friend at work" are not only more likely to be happier and healthier, they are also seven times as likely to be engaged in their jobs. What's more, employees who report having friends at work have higher levels of productivity, retention, and job satisfaction than those who don't.

Research shows that, after food and shelter, belonging is a fundamental human need. Given that we spend between eight and nine hours of our day at work (not including commute time), we have significantly less time to fulfill our social needs outside of work. When we're not working, we're either dealing with family, running errands, or trying to grab some rest when we can.

The workplace, where we spend such a large portion of our time, is an ideal place to foster the positive connections we all need — not just for our well-being, but also for our productivity and health.

A case study: Hollister Construction Services

Chris Johnson of Hollister Construction Services in Parsippany, NJ., is a member of a group of CEOs with whom I worked five years ago. He took me aside and asked: "Can you do this with my executive team?" In the half decade since, I've conducted cultural integration sessions with every one of his now 200 employees.

The culture at Hollister is like a big family. When they created a word cloud of how the employees describe the culture, the word "family" was clearly the biggest. See for yourself.

This word cloud is a testament to the amazing culture we have cultivated at Hollister by unleashing the power of friends at work. Here's what some of their employees say about their personal experiences after harnessing this power.

- ❖ Andrew, Senior Estimator – "If I'm not getting along with someone, I'm not inspired to work at all, or I'm just fighting to get through the day. The work is just a manifestation of your sense of ease and comfort with your team."

- ❖ Allison, Assistant Project Manager – "I don't come to work looking for friends but having a close friend at work makes a better day, and I'm more productive because I'm happier. Having someone with whom to discuss my struggles and knowing that they get it is very helpful."

❖ Tina, NY Operations – "Friends in whom you can confide make the day go faster. It's easier to work together. These friendships have developed naturally and some-times through team-building events."

❖ Sam, VP Finance – "Having friend-ships formed here makes it very hard to leave here. It keeps the place going. We bond together to get through hard times."

❖ Ed, Project Executive – " The culture promotes friendships. That creates trust, which in turn allows open conversations. That culture starts from the top."

❖ Edison, Senior Project Manager – "When you spend 10 hours a day with people you care for, it's not a job. It's like being a family. You do more for friends than other people – you go the extra mile."

❖ Christina, Assistant Project Manager – "This company has become my family. I've never felt so excited to come to a place every day. All of us coming together to learn and create this culture has also helped me personally. We want to help each other grow, and it starts with our CEO."

❖ Ann Marie, Receptionist/Office Support – "I go above and beyond because of friendship. I have their backs and they have mine, and that is comforting, reassuring and powerful. Having someone with whom you can laugh, and cry allows you to blow off steam and decompress the situation."

A Tech Guru on the Symbiosis of Friendship and Culture

I had the opportunity to interview Jeff Marowits on the relationship between friendship and corporate culture. Jeff is a partner at Keystone Strategy Partners, whose clients have included tech giants such as Amazon, Facebook and LinkedIn. Some of his words are transcribed below, verbatim.

Friendship and culture is an interesting topic . . . A team that has interpersonal trust and professional trust (which are different) [is] a team that can withstand a lot of challenge.

In some cultures, professional settings require friendship first. That's not the

American culture. It's viewed as salesy or schmoozy and not connoting quality. The only way I've seen to solve it is through consistency. Go in slow chunks and build from there.

I think friendship is positively correlated with happiness and productivity in the workplace. It's more positively correlated with being able to stand the slings and arrows of difficult situations. When you've been in the trenches, it deepens the bond but I would suggest that the bond deepens the ability to battle. When we are friends, we're willing to do a lot for one another when things are a little tougher and when people are stretched or when you're going to ask someone what they need to do.

I like to include people with my family. I don't see a division between personal and professional. . . . I'm going home at

5 pm tomorrow and I'm having dinner with my family, so inviting someone to join me doesn't detract from time with my family. This is with a close client, not an obligation. I view it all as additive, not a zero sum game.

Takeaway

The research is clear: workplace friendships are an important and powerful force both for the employees and the employers. In the chapters to follow we will look at the Seven Keys to friendship and how to affect this change in your organization.

Tom Rath

Jim Harter

LinkedIn's Relationships @ Work Study

O.C. Tanner

Chapter

Judgment-Free

"We learned that if we want to get close to someone, we share our truth (good, bad and ugly) rather than pass judgment by offering advice and opinion"

Mo Fathelbab, *Forum: The Secret Advantage of Successful Leaders*

To me, "judgment free" means making a commitment to myself that I won't be so self-important as to believe that I know what's best for another.

When I wrote my first book, *Forum: The Secret Advantage of Successful Leaders*, I thoroughly covered this concept from the perspective of the workings of peer groups. At the time, the notion of "don't judge me" was alive, but not as much as it is today. You'll hear the words "not judging" from many people, starting with teenagers.

In this book, I focus on the impact judgment has on relationships, how to recognize when we are being judgmental (it's not always obvious) and how not to fall into a common trap.

The Hidden Costs of Judging

Simply put, judgment of another person can be hurtful. Feeling judged by someone you love hurts even more, because that person matters! While the person judging you is not trying to be hurtful, his/her judgmental comment impacts you emotionally.

You may not say anything at the time, but the experience teaches you to be more guarded and cautious with that person. You now know that being exposed or expressing vulnerability with the person may put your emotional wellbeing at risk.

What that means in plain words is that you begin to hide parts of yourself or your truth. You reduce your vulnerability with that person because he/she has violated you. The result, of course, is more of a surface relationship than a robust one.

By way of example, back in the 90s I was in a relationship that was not in a good place. I needed to move on, but I simply did not have the courage to break up with my girlfriend. While I was riding this emotional roller-coaster one of my best friends, with all good intentions, began to give me advice upon advice that I should break up with this girl.

It was the right advice, but that didn't help. I needed someone to help me process my emotions. I needed someone to share a similar experience, by saying something like: "I've been there and it sucked! I had lots of doubts and it was painful. Even after the breakup, I had second thoughts."

This approach would have given me the message I needed to hear and would have brought me closer to my friend as he expressed his own challenge and vulnerability. Instead, what happened is that I eventually broke up with my ex-girlfriend and my friend.

The Judgment Trap

It's easy to recognize judgment when you are the recipient, because you feel it. The emotional impact is clear. What is tougher is recognizing when we are judging others. Even if we say nothing, we often express judgment that sometimes manifests in unspoken ways.

These unspoken judgments are even more tricky, because without words the judge's intentions maybe misconstrued. Say, for example, your friend rolls his eyes as you're telling a story. That can be a judgment of you, or it can be a judgment of the person in your story.

By all means, if you can exercise the benefit of the doubt, and you sincerely won't hold onto it as a judgment, that is great. On the other hand, if you are feeling judged and you're not able to let it go, check it out with your friend. He may not be aware of the eye roll or may have intended it for the other person and not you.

Other non-verbal judgments can be a sigh, a gasp, crossing your arms, squinting your eyes and aligning something in the distance or simply shaking your head.

Verbal judgments can come in the form of a question. One of my clients shared a way to detect those questions that has become my favorite: "If you can add the word 'idiot' at the end of a question, you're being judgmental."

Consider these questions:

Why did you do that?

Don't you think you should have done this instead?

Wouldn't it be better if you did that?

Although tone is critical, each one, innocuous as it appears on the surface, may be strapped with potentially explosive judgment.

Another place that's ripe for judgment is advice, as in:

> This is what you should do. . . .

> Here's what I would do if I were you. . . .

> You ought to do this. . . .

> My advice to you is to. . . .

Don't get me wrong: there are times when advice is sought, and advice is given and it's all good. I'm simply pointing out that it's a risky proposition. Instead of advice, I've found speaking from experience to be far more respectful, accurate (if specific), humble, vulnerable, equalizing and connecting.

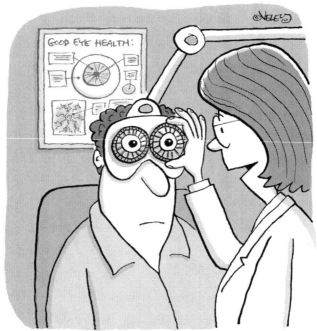

"Now let's talk about that disastrous business decision you made ten years ago. I want to see if your hindsight has improved since your last check-up!"

CartoonStock.com

Takeaway

People ask for advice all the time, and that can become a judgment trap. Not knowing what the person who just asked for my advice really wants, my first question is: "What's going on?" My next question is: "How can I help?" or more specifically, "Which of these three requests reflects what you want?"

Can you help me figure it out?

Can you share how you've handled this issue in the past or how you handle it presently?

I need you to listen and really hear what happened and how I'm feeling.

I cannot imagine someone's actually wanting advice more than \wanting to find an answer. Being judgment free prevents us from confusing the two.

Chapter

Mischievous Fun

Mischievous: *def.* "playful, reckless behavior that is not intended to cause serious harm."

Fun: *def.* "someone or something that is amusing or enjoyable; an enjoyable experience or person; an enjoyable or amusing time; the feeling of being amused or entertained"

Merriam-Webster Dictionary

This chapter is perhaps the one that I've been most excited about writing and also the riskiest, especially as it relates to the workplace! I doubt that you'll find another book espousing mischief as a tool for friendship. But if you think about your closest friends for a moment and think about something mischievous that you did together, it will all fall into place.

Remember How to Have Fun

On many appropriate occasions I have asked groups of CEOs to share something mischievous they did as children, and there has never been a shortage of stories.

It could be as simple as a little prank that you played on April Fools Day. Something about that experience and sharing that laugh or giggle has the power to bond us. I would dare say that the more mischievous, the more fun!

I have many such memories that I cherish. As kids, we used to put big firecrackers in trash cans and watch the tops blow off as the M80s exploded.

A few years later on a rainy day some friends and I were driving by a bus stop, and there were many people waiting for the bus. As we approached the bus stop, we saw a puddle and we purposefully drove into it, splashing a few people with the murky water.

While it was not nice to the people at the bus stop, we laughed so hard we were in tears! Thirty years later we still laugh when we recount the story. This is also my opportunity to publicly apologize to those who were drenched— I'm truly sorry!

How to Have Fun with Friends at Work

My own experience, professionally and personally, is that bonding happens in many ways, and fun is one of those keys not to be neglected. If you can't have fun with your friends, you need new friends!

Here are a few examples of how to build bonds with colleagues that will come back in spades when times at work get tough.

We've all been to many a long, boring dinner. Instead of simply sitting around waiting to be served, have someone host the dinner and organize a cooking competition. Pair people up to work on different dishes and then create different prizes like *Most Creative, Best in Show, Best Presentation,* etc.

My better half and her team went caroling after the holiday dinner — that was fun!

Bring in some board games and give people an opportunity to play. Play and fun tend to go hand in hand.

One of our clients took their team to a go-kart track. That was fun and really gave a sense of the personalities on the team in very short order. You can see who is competitive and who is afraid, who has to win and who doesn't care. It was fun and illuminating.

Takeaway

If you're going to make friends at work, by all means have some fun. Far be it from me to define what's fun for someone else. Do what works for you, whether it's having a drink, playing golf, going to dinner, going to a game or a concert or even going on a trip. The list is endless. Get creative and have some fun!

Chapter

Vulnerability

"Vulnerability is the currency of relationships. Without vulnerability relationships remain superficial."

David Bradford, professor at Stanford Graduate School of Business and author of *Power Up.*

"The hardest thing about being a leader is demonstrating or showing vulnerability. . . . When the leader demonstrates vulnerability and sensibility and brings people together, the team wins."

Howard Schultz. Former CEO and executive chairman of Starbucks.

I first heard David Bradford's words when I was attending a certification program that he co-led. To me, they represented a brilliant way to express a concept that I'd been living professionally for well over 15 years but had never been able to express so effectively.

It took me many years to develop this insight through my work with CEO peer groups. I saw a powerful bonding force that was inexplicable in social situations to which I'd been accustomed.

But it was only later in life that I learned to dig below the surface and make the sorts of genuine connections with colleagues, friends and loved ones that lead to true friendship. Only when I began to open myself up and take risks was I able to reap these rewards. These durable friendships have proven to me time and again the true power of vulnerability.

Being Real

Someone else who expanded my understanding of this concept was Bernie Tenenbaum, managing partner of Lodestone Global and also managing partner of China Cat Capital, LLC. Bernie once told me, "It's possible to be vulnerable and not be authentic."

Because I respect Bernie so deeply, I thought about his words for a long time. I'd taken it for granted that vulnerability included authenticity. But he made me realize that just opening up is not enough. We must make a commitment to dig deeply and share our emotions honestly.

Bernie's comment persuaded me to add the word "authenticity" to my personal definition. The great irony is that being both vulnerable and true to oneself is how we achieve the strongest connection to others.

Disclosure Equals Connection

In my work with CEO peer groups and executive teams, I have found the most effective way to build trust and real relationships is to create opportunities for deep disclosure. What often struck me in doing this work was how often someone would say: "I've never shared this with anyone before"; or "You guys now know more about me than my own family does."

Sometimes I've even heard: "I feel closer to this group than I do to my best friends. This is real." While some people feel apprehensive before deeply sharing, almost without exception afterwards they feel lighter or relieved and they always feel more connected.

So, what prevents us from having this kind of authenticity with our family and friends? Having learned what is possible as I witnessed the results of authentic/ vulnerable sharing among even the most senior corporate peer groups, that is a question that I immediately began to ponder. Soon, the answers started to reveal themselves.

Rewards of Risk

Discussed elsewhere in this book you'll find more about non-judgment, condentiality and trust, truth, commitment and fun. All of these concepts worked so well in my work with more than 20,000 CEOs and also proved to work in most of my own relationships. Eureka! I thought, at a certain point in my life. I have struck gold! Or had I?

My own vulnerability was only one side of the equation. In the words of David Bradford, there's the perennial problem of the chicken and the egg. Who goes first?

To further complicate matters, there is the real possibility that I put myself out and the person doesn't reciprocate.

That is a risk that you have to assess. I cannot tell you or make you take that risk. By definition, vulnerability is risky. In fact, if I'm not taking a risk I'm not being vulnerable.

Once when she was being interviewed by Oprah Winfrey, Brené Brown (author of *The Power of Vulnerability, Daring Greatly, The Gift of Imperfection* and *Braving the Wilderness*) turned the tables and questioned Oprah about this point. Oprah's answer was: "The price of vulnerability is that there will be times when someone takes advantage of you." Oprah, please forgive me if I misquoted your exact words, but that is the gist of it.

Strong Leaders Set the Tone

In Patrick Lencioni's best-selling book, *The 5 Dysfunctions of a Team,* he writes about trust as the basis for healthy conflict, commitment, accountability and attention to results. He says to share personal histories to build trust and strongly recommends that in a corporate setting the CEO should be the first to do so, in that way setting the example and showing the way for the rest of the team.

I know many CEOs for whom that is a scary proposition. I know many others who embrace the notion that showing their true humanity not only connects them with their teams, but also sets a tone and the culture for the whole organization.

The ways these leaders choose to open up vary, but at the core the approach works because people are willing to be vulnerable, not just in sharing openly but also in speaking their truth. More about that later.

How We (Inadvertently) Block Vulnerability

Brené Brown's TED talk, "The Power of Vulnerability," has collected more than 35 million views. I love that talk so much that I've watched and listened to it many times. From Brené and others, I've learned that sometimes we block vulnerability without being aware of it. What we're doing, in effect, shuts down someone's attempt to open up. Here are some ways that happens:

Interrupting – Sometimes someone is just warming up, and when we interrupt we make it less safe or simply don't give that person the time to express what they wish to.

Speaking too quickly – As conversations get deeper, it's really important to pay attention to the pace. You know this intuitively. When something is serious, people slow down. If we feel the need to speak as soon as the other person is finished talking, we are not honoring the power of silence and giving the person an opportunity to continue.

Jokes and humor – This is the easy eject button when a conversation gets uncomfortable. It's understandable. It's certainly more fun to laugh than to get into deep and painful subjects. Comfortable as it may be, this defense mechanism is also a lethal weapon against vulnerability.

Dismissal – This is when we dismiss the issue altogether or dispute its existence. It's like your mom saying, "You're not ugly?" or "I wouldn't worry about it."

Trivializing – "It's no big deal."

Rescuing – Playing the hero is a big temptation for many people, but fixing someone's problem or saving them is not always helpful. It causes the person to rely upon you and it shuts down further exploration and the deeper conversation.

Asking the wrong questions – In addition to questions that fall into the category of judgment and advice as covered in that chapter, I want to point out that the person asking *any* question is not being vulnerable, while pushing the other person into being vulnerable. Have you ever been to lunch with someone and found that he or she asked you questions for the entire time? That person shared nothing about him/ herself, while you spilled your guts.

Advice – Again this is a subject important enough to merit a separate chapter (see Chapter Two – Judgment Free).

Takeaway

People are aching for authentic friends. We are wired for human connection, and sometimes we just need a tool, an excuse or someone to simply tell us it's okay to reach out and be vulnerable.

Master the skill of digging below the surface to make those genuine connections with colleagues, friends and loved ones that lead to true friendship. And learn to avoid well-intentioned behaviors that block connection.

David L. Bradford

Bernard Tenenbaum

Brené Brown

Patrick Lencioni

Chapter

Kind Truth

"Holding anger and saying or doing nothing about it is like drinking poison and hoping the other person will die."

Versions of this quote have been attributed to various authors, religious leaders, even Alcoholics Anonymous. I believe Mahatma Gandhi was the first to say these words.

"If there's a pile of shit in the middle of the table you can ignore it and let it stink or you can use it for fertilizer and grow something beautiful."

Delbert White, an old Texan

After a number of years working with entrepreneurs and creating hundreds of peer groups, I realized that there was an uncomfortable subject that I found myself consistently either avoiding or ignoring. That subject is one of the inevitable aspects of life: conflict.

Much of my perception of conflict at that time was negative. I realized that I was a natural conflict avoider. To me, the concept of "clearing the air" was not merely foreign. It was ugly and scary, a real lose-lose.

However, I realized that not engaging productively at this level was limiting my ability to effect change. In 2000, I joined a new community of peer practitioners with whom I learned about a process called "clearing the air."

After a couple of years of experimentation, I became convinced of its importance and its efficacy. I saw a powerful change in the quality of communication in terms of honesty, vulnerability and ultimately deep connection.

Still there were times when the clearing process did not go so well. Something went wrong, and the results were not as favorable as I'd hoped. The conversation was not safe or fruitful. I began to think about what had gone wrong. I started to see patterns, which led me to a simple exercise that had a big impact.

Difficult Conversations Happen

This exercise started out as a conversation in which I asked a group of CEOs or an executive team the following question: "What are the responsibilities of each party, the sender and the receiver, in a difficult conversation, in order for that conversation to be productive, effective and respectful?"

Over time — years, in fact — I began to recognize (and frankly be quite surprised at) the consistency of responses to my question. What is powerful about this conversation with any team is that it creates a shared agreement reflecting not one person's view but that of all members of the team.

I have now come to realize that often we, as leaders, have gotten where we are despite a less-than- optimal approach to difficult conversations. My sincere hope is that, armed with this Key, you'll see value for a new approach to conflict in all facets of your life and that "Kind Truth" will allow you and your teams to experience far less pain with or avoidance of difficult conversations.

How Do You Clear the Air?

Clearing the air is beautifully explained in the landmark book by Harville Hendrix, Getting the Love You Want. This book has been the basis for Amago Couples Therapy and for many workplace conversations.

STEP 1. Ask for permission to ensure that it is the right time and place. Once permission has been granted, the sender (the person who has an issue to clear) moves on to Step 2, stating things as s/he sees observes the situation.

STEP 2. The sender completes an inventory by stating the following things, as s/he sees them.

Facts - The observable facts

Feelings - The emotions

Judgments - The story or stories I make up about the situation.

My part, my role, my baggage, why I am affected

Want - My goal in this conversation.

STEP 3. The receiver (the person with whom someone has an issue to clear) must reflect back or mirror what s/he has heard. The purpose of this step is to show the sender that s/he has been heard. Sometimes that alone is enough to resolve the situation.

Another reason is to avoid any miscommunication. How many times have you been in an argument that took a turn because one party misheard something that was said?

STEP 4. The receiver asks, "Is that right?" (Did I get your message) And "Is there more?" (Is there something else).

Note, it is important that the clearing the air conversation deals with one issue at a time. If either party has more, each of those items is handled as a separate issue in order to avoid piling on and to allow both parties to be clean (not holding tension toward the other person) at the end of the conversation.

The Sender's Responsibilities

Remember this is a toolbox for a lifetime. Give yourself permission to experiment with different tools. Using them will increase your ability to turn difficult conversations into opportunities for personal and professional growth.

Be prepared: As you'll see in the following points, there is a lot to take into account in having a productive conversation. Spending the appropriate time to develop clarity is important. It may take five minutes or an hour, but either way preparation is key.

Start with an expression of love : Remember that you are using this process because you actually care and/or have a stake in this relationship. If you don't care about this relationship, please look elsewhere for how you address this person. I like to say: "We clear because we care."

State facts: Sometimes the facts are hard to come by, but without the facts the receiver has no prayer of understanding what you are trying to convey. "You don't believe me" is not a fact; it's a judgment. "You rolled your eyes" is a fact.

Own judgments: This is a controversial point in that some would say (as do I) one should not judge, or we should suspend judgment. The truth is that we have judgments, and they may very well have nothing to do with the truth. Judgments are simply the stories we make up about the situation.

For the sender, the value in recognizing the judgments is the realization that they are not facts. If you are late, that is a fact. If I conclude that you do not consider this meeting important enough to warrant your timeliness, that, of course, is just a judgment and has no factual basis.

State your emotions, NOT your wrath: It is important for the receiver to understand and for the sender to express the emotional impact of the situation. Owning emotion and naming it is valuable for both parties.

Of course, when the sender is very emotional the receiver can feel attacked. As John Gottman (*The Seven Principles of*

Making Marriage Work) puts it, s/he can also "feel flooded." Being flooded is like being overwhelmed and thus unable to hear/receive any more.

While it might be difficult for you to see another's point of view, it's important to remember that our emotions are our truth. There is no wrong emotion for either party. Even if the facts are not exactly right, how I feel is how I feel.

State your part: As the sender, you may feel that you have nothing to do with the situation that triggered an emotion for you. In reality, the fact that you reacted emotionally to the situation means that you do indeed have a part.

When John is late to the meeting, that may not be a trigger for everyone. Different people may have different emotions about it. How each person is affected is all about that person. Joe may be angry because he missed his kid's ballgame to be on time, while Sue may have no negative reaction at all because John is her friend. Figuring out your part and stating it helps deepen the understanding of the situation for both parties.

State your want: To clear the air with someone and to not have a want is a way of attacking that person. If you have no want, you essentially refuse to accept any remedy. Your want can be to be heard, to be understood, an apology, a promise to try to change or anything else.

Of course, your want may be unreasonable, and the other person may not be able to give you what you want, but for the sake of you as sender communicating your issue, it's important that you have a want.

Be clear: When the sender is vague, the receiver is in the dark. The receiver is not able to demonstrate effectively that he or she has heard the situation or to modify his/her behavior.

As the sender, you are not helping by beating around the bush. Be specific, refer to specific situations and try not to generalize.

Be concise: Being concise lets the receiver actually hear and absorb what is being conveyed. Rambling on makes it nearly impossible for the receiver to hear or demonstrate hearing and is often a form of attack in and of itself.

Be timely: The longer you hold on to the issue, the more it builds up and the more likely you'll erupt. Once you've recognized the issue and have been able to organize your thoughts and express them calmly, you are ready to approach the receiver.

Be respectful: Clearing the air is about maintaining and building a trusting relationship. Without respect, neither building nor maintaining is possible.

Do not use this process as a tool with which to attack. If your intention is to attack someone, please do not use any of the tools or labels in this book.

Be open to the possibility that you may be wrong: As the sender, you may have built up a case of which you are so convinced that you fail to see the whole story. One little detail can change that story entirely.

Be vulnerable: Having a clearing conversation requires vulnerability by both parties, but the sender is being vulnerable in bringing up the issue, stating his/her facts, feelings, judgments, his/ her part in the situation, and what s/he wants from the receiver. This vulnerability can be uncomfortable and is perhaps why so many of us avoid conflict in the first place.

Understand that you may not be able to get what you want : A want is sometimes a request for a change in behavior on the part of the receiver. This change may be something of which the receiver is simply incapable. Maybe the receiver just suffered a loss and is uncontrollably crying. Just because the sender wants the receiver to stop crying doesn't mean the receiver is able to just stop.

Recognize that it is your issue: This is a fundamental and important part of this process. If the other person is late and it bothers me, it is my problem. That is, at least until I say something, at which point others may share that problem, but it is always my problem because it bothers me.

Look for growth opportunity for yourself and for the relationship: I have grown in many ways through conversations like these. The first is getting comfortable with being able to do it more often. Another is a deeper understanding of myself and my triggers. A third is getting comfortable enough to ask for what I want or need.

Be willing to let go of the issue and of changing the receiver: Clearing the air is not about holding a grudge. It may be hard to do in certain situations, but letting go is the ideal intent.

Consider the setting: Private or public? I don't believe there's a right or wrong answer for all situations, but I do think there are factors that impact this decision. These factors include personalities, impact on a team, volatility of the situation, potential embarrassment and timing.

In peer groups and executive teams, clearing the air within the group creates trust for the group as a whole. It helps other members of the team clear by proxy. It reinforces the process, creates more comfort and acceptance of the process, and highlights issues that may impact the team as a whole. Remember, this is not a public attack. It is the sender's problem after all.

Consider the location and medium: Texting, messaging or email are not options. Phone may be okay. In person is best.

Consider timing for you and the receiver: Some issues require more time. Five minutes before an important appointment is probably not be the best time to have a conversation.

Consider your body language and facial expressions: Sometimes our words are not aligned with our body language or facial expression. I would venture to guess that is because we're not being truthful or because we're completely unaware of how we come across.

Remember this is about the quality of the relationship: The clearing model is not intended in any way to be used to harm a relationship. Of course, there is no guarantee that because you use the model it will work every time. There are situations that simply cannot be overcome, and no communication model will be the panacea.

Be specific and don't generalize: One area that can lead to difficulty in difficult conversations is what occurs when the receiver has no connection to the sender's message. In order to avoid any confusion, it's critical to be a specific as possible.

Do not criticize the person; focus on the behavior: A behavior is not about who the person "is." It's about what the person "does." By criticizing who the person is, we risk hurting that person's feelings from the start of the conversation and even closing it down before it gets started. Saying something like, "You are an idiot" or "You are dumb" is a judgment and in insult. Instead, one might say, "When you asked me to stay home, I felt left out." That speaks to a specific behavior.

Listen: This may be surprising to some people, but even the sender has to listen— on many levels, including:

1. What is the receiver's reaction?

2. Is there a possibility of a mis-understanding on the sender's part?

3. How did the sender feel as s/he heard himself/herself speaking about something difficult?

Use neutral language: Words like "never" and "always" can leave the receiver feeling attacked. A better way is to say something like, "when you do this. . . . "

The Receiver's Responsibilities

Like the sender, the receiver can master certain skills that will improve the outcomes of difficult conversations. Keep in mind, the process of acquiring these skills is part of our life's journey. They cannot all be absorbed—or acquired— in a single try.

Listen and hear: Listening is a whole science. David Clutterbuck (author of *Everyone Needs a Mentor* and more than 50 books on the subject of mentoring) provides a construct for five levels of listening that is very instructive:

❖ Listening to disagree

❖ Listening while waiting for your turn to speak

❖ Listening to understand

❖ Listening to help the other person understand

❖ Listening without intent

Generally, using the description of the five levels of listening is designed to create awareness for mentor/mentee relationships. In our case, the receiver will best serve the clearing process by listening to understand.

Listening to understand includes lis-tening for the emotions and paying attention to body language. People feel truly heard when we hear their emotions and their facts, not just the facts.

Look for the gift: This is perhaps a growth opportunity. It is likely that the receiver's behavior in a given situation is replicated in other situations and with other people. When the receiver can look for the gift, the conversation becomes a powerful oppor-tunity.

Try to understand: Demonstrate your listening by confirming what you heard.

Be respectful: The clearing conversation is NOT a fight or an argument and cer-tainly not war. Remember, this is about improving a relationship.

Don't be defensive: Instead of focusing on defending your position, focus on deeply understanding the sender. Remember this conversation is as much about the sender as it is about you.

One way that defensiveness undermines this is when the receiver refutes the example given by the sender and uses that as a way to derail the conversation.

Don't use as an opportunity to attack: This should go without saying. Remember, you can always put up your boundary or ask for more time if need be. If the time is not right, the place is not good or you're being flooded (overwhelmed), just ask if you can have this conversation at another time.

Recognize the sender's emotions are always right: This is a golden rule of life. For any situation, people will have different emotions and for every one of those people, their emotions are their emotions and we cannot take that away from them. When someone tries to deny us our feelings we feel invalidated, which only makes matters worse.

Notice your own emotions: Your emotions are valid as well. By all means demonstrate hearing the sender completely before sharing how you feel about the situation.

Recognize the risk/vulnerability required for the sender: The sender is taking a risk in having this conversation with you. How you "receive" will not only affect the sender in the moment, but it will also affect your level of trust and the sender's ability and willingness to be honest with you in future situations.

Ask clarifying questions if needed: If you don't understand what the sender is saying, ask for a specific example.

Takeaway

Difficult conversations are a part of life, and must be appreciated as opportunities for growth rather than avoided. Practice the four-step technique outlined in this chapter known as "Clearing the Air," recognizing that the purpose is to be heard and understood.

Often clearing the air can lead to a resolution, but expecting that it will lead to a resolution can sometimes be unrealistic. There are a vast array of tools for both sender and receiver, the mastery of which over time will promote the likelihood of a positive resolution.

Harville Hendrix

John Gottman

David Clutterbuck

Chapter

Reliability

"When friendships are real, they are not glass threads or frost work, but the solidest things we can know."

Ralph Waldo Emerson, *Essays: First Series*

"It has always been my contention that an individual who can be relied upon to be himself and to be honest unto himself can be relied upon in every other way."

J. Paul Getty, *How to Be Rich*

"At least you always know exactly where you are
with Fred, he ALWAYS lets you down!"

Think about your best friends. I'll bet
they are trustworthy and they perform
consistently well. Trust means a lot of
different things to different people. For

some, trust is a given until it's violated. For others, trust must be earned.

We've all had friends who have let us down. They've not showed up, or they have left us in an uncomfortable situation, or they didn't call back, or they dusted us for someone else, or they had a pattern that said, "You cannot count on me." We've also had friends violate our confidentiality by sharing with someone else and saying something like, "Oh, but it's confidential."

A real friend will not only be there as planned, but will also drop anything to be there for you in time of need. This aspect of friendship is so important that my colleagues and I have built it into the structure of our work with corporate leaders who participate in forums.

Forums Are Built on Trust

CEO Forums are groups of 8-10 CEOs who meet regularly in a structured confidential environment to help each other grow personally and professionally. In these groups, the rules are clear. If you miss two meetings in one year, you are out! That is unless you have great excuse, and the group unanimously votes you back in.

That may sound punitive, but I promise you that for the last 27 years I have gone to my CEO Forum meetings because I want to, not because I have to. I think I've missed fewer than 5 meetings in those 27 years. So why do we have such rules?

Because we learned the hard way that unless we had a clear expectation we were subject to different interpretations of what it means to be committed.

A very important part of the effectiveness of this rule is that we all agreed to it, and it was not imposed on anyone. It was merely suggested as a best practice. To that end, some groups do not apply this practice either by having lower standards or by having no agreement at all. The groups with no agreement at all suffer the most because of a lack of clarity of expectations.

Clear Expectations

So how does all this translate to friendships and other real relationships? I can tell you that I can think of several situations in which I lost a best friend because we had different expectations. Two of them wanted me to not to have any other friends. Perhaps they were jealous, I don't know. I wanted them to be part of a larger group of friends.

In hindsight, I realize that those friends wanted more of me than I was willing or able to give at the time. Their concept of friendship was different from mine. I'm not sure I could have had this conversation back then without hurting someone's feelings. Now, I am more aware of this dynamic, and I'm careful to engage accordingly so as not to repeat the pattern.

In other words, I'm clear on what my expectations are and that has been more than half the battle in keeping me out of confusing situations. Perhaps in the eyes of those friends I was not reliable!

What Is Confidentiality?

Reliability also means that you won't betray my trust. If I share something with you in confidence, you won't betray me and share it with someone else.

Confidentiality is the cornerstone of the CEO Forums, and what became apparent to me very quickly is that for many people this sanctuary is one of the few places and sometimes the only place where we can trust in the confidentiality.

Confidentiality is also the cornerstone of team-building meetings. If we are to build a team and trusting relationships, confidentiality is simply a must as it relates to personal sharing and keeping our confidentiality agreements.

Indeed, in the real world, confidentiality means different things to different people. For some it means I will tell my spouse, because I tell her/him everything. For others it means I will tell one other person, but I will tell them it's confidential.

That's certainly not my definition of confidentiality. Until people in a group are

100 percent clear on how confidentiality is defined and until there is complete trust, there is no safety to share openly. Until we share openly, relationships remain superficial.

Being Honest About Trust

The sad part of this tale is that once our confidentiality is violated, not only do we become guarded with the person who betrayed our trust, we also become guarded in general.

It is hard to keep a secret, and we've all slipped at some point. I certainly have slipped, but it's been a long, long time since it happened. The consequences are too grave. Even more sad is that too often we say nothing to the offender and the relationship suffers as we just write it off.

What if, in fact, my friend did not violate my confidentiality and there was a real misunderstanding on my part? What if I made an assumption that my friend violated my confidentiality when in fact it was someone else? Addressing the issue is critical, because even if I don't get peace in my heart, at least I will have an honest relationship with my friend and no one is left wondering what happened.

Takeaway

Trust is the basis of relationships. Work to establish clear, shared expectations, and make sure that all parties understand and agree to the same definition of confidentiality.

Chapter

Sharing and Generosity

"People come either from 'givington' or 'takington'."

Maria Sipka, serial entrepreneur and Co-Founder and VP of Brand Strategy at Linqia

"We make a living by what we get, but we make a life by what we give.

Winston Churchill

Real friends will share what they have. If I have one sandwich between my friend and me, I cannot imagine not giving half of that sandwich to my friend. That is the spirit of sharing and generosity.

"Sharing is saying you're my friend, without having to say 'you're my friend'."

Givers and Takers

Maria Sipka's simple categories prompt each of us to consider: Where are we from? In other words: How do we interact with others? I would also then ask, what sort of person should I surround myself with?

Because I think of myself as coming from givington, I've realized that I must surround myself with people that also come from givington.

For someone who is a giver, being surrounded by takers gets old quickly. That certainly begs the question: what if you are a taker? I can't imagine that a bunch of takers can get along that well either, as they all vie to take from one another.

That leads me to believe that takers must take from givers. That might work for some time, but eventually it has to lead to resentment and the giver's feeling that the taker is taking advantage.

As a giver, I might also wonder if the taker is genuinely more interested in my friendship or in what I'm giving.

Real Relationships Require Generosity

Within real relationships, generosity is contagious, as I discovered firsthand some years ago. I'd heard that one of my friends was cheap and stingy from more than one source. My experience with this friend was quite the opposite. I found him extremely generous with me. Of course, I am extremely generous with him. Giving begets more giving!

By contrast, I can think of another friend who was very cheap and stingy in every sense. At the time I recognized this, it seemed to be centered around money.

Now that I think about it, it was a pervasive attitude of not giving. People with a scarcity mentality find it hard to give when they think they don't have enough and that's understandable to a point.

How to Give

Generosity is not just about money It starts with an attitude of giving and what follows can show up in a variety of ways. Here are just a few examples.

Time is the greatest gift we can give a friend. Especially when that friend is in need.

Sharing information is another form of generosity. When a friend sends me an article in which he believes I'll be interested, it tells me that he is thinking about me.

Hosting friends is another form of generosity. It doesn't have to be elaborate, but it's a way of giving and sharing and letting someone into your life.

Connecting others for their benefit is another way of demonstrating our care for others and is an act of generosity.

Compliments make our friends feel better and certainly are an act of generosity.

Hugs are a physical way of expressing caring and are a form of generosity.

Paying Attention

As you can see, not giving because you have no money is no excuse. Attention to another is a way of saying you care and that this friend is important. There are many other ways to give.

Cooking a meal for someone is an act of love. Just offering a taste of what is on your plate is an act of generosity.

Offering to give a ride is a simple way of being generous with your time and your resources.

Fixing something for a friend shows you care. You are giving your time, your talent and yourself.

Giving a painting if you are an artist is another form of generosity. My mother has been extremely generous, and this is just one of the ways that she has shown her love and generosity.

Giving a music cd or playlist is another way of saying "I'm thinking about you." That is certainly very generous.

Bringing a meal when someone is unable to make their own or just because you felt like it or as a contribution when you're invited to a friend's house is a clear act of giving. A rule I try to live by is to always bring something when I visit a friend. Sometimes I'm unable, and in those situations I bring my thanks, appreciation and gratitude.

Walking a friend's dog maybe when he's sick or travelling is another way of expressing your generosity.

Helping a friend with a project is another act of giving.

While these examples can be thought of for existing friendships, if you think about it, you may even realize that you have some friendships that developed as a result of an act of generosity.

Takeaway

Real relationships are based on giving, and thrive on a spirit of generosity. Gifts need not be expensive to be meaningful. Sometimes, time spent with a friend is the greatest gift of all. Start with asking yourself, am I from *Givington* or *Takington?*

Chapter

Shared Purpose

and Values

"I have three messages. One is we should never, ever give up. Two is you are never too old to chase your dreams. And three is it looks like a solitary sport, but it takes a team."

Diana Nyad, at age 64 and on her 5th try in 35 years, became the first person to swim from Cuba to Florida without a shark cage

Some of my closest and most enduring friendships were either forged or strengthened because we had a common goal.

A number of years ago, a group of us decided to do an Ironman triathlon. This would require us to swim 2.4 miles, bike 112 miles, and then run a full (26.2-mile) marathon. And I can assure you, that last .2 matters because at that point, every inch is a struggle.

The competition we entered took place in Switzerland, and was the first Ironman for all but one of us. Generally, completing the Ironman can take as much as 17 hours, or if you are a world-class competitor just over 8 hours. Our tribe all came in around the 14-hour mark, an accomplishment of which we were all very proud.

To this day, my triathlete friends and I share a special bond. Of course, this bond did not just develop as a result of one race. We spent hundreds of hours training, competing in smaller triathlons and marathons, traveling for those events and having fun along the way.

When we decided to take on this challenge, we didn't do it in order to deepen our friendships. Nonetheless, in hindsight I believe it was a powerful factor in the deep bonds that we created. In some ways undertaking such a grueling event was like going to war for us. It gives me a glimpse of what incredible bonds soldiers build, especially if they go to combat together. Of course we had very little concern for our lives, but there were times when a bike accident was very scary.

Growing the
Entrepreneurs Organization

Another example is that of the amazing team that built the Entrepreneurs Organization (EO) from 1990-1997. (Members of this group must have founded a business that has at least $1,000,000 in annual sales revenue.) This team was composed of staff and volunteers who took EO from 100 members to 2000 members during those years. It was a great journey that was full of challenges.

My role was associate director for the first year and then executive director for the last six years. As of this writing in August of 2018, the organization has more than 13,000 members in 53 countries.

Over the course of countless board meetings, chapter launches, conferences, and training events, a group of us did something special. We made a difference and had fun along the way.

What's truly magical is that to this day, some 21 years later, we have unbreakable bonds and even though we are scattered around the world we have an instant and real connection when we get together.

We had a shared purpose to build the leading global organization for entrepreneurs. It was a bold goal that in my opinion has been achieved. We never could have done it without the buy-in of all the members of our team.

Shared Purpose

Elizabeth Trigg also worked at EO after I left for a number of years. We have continued our relationship to this day. She's been a Godsend for the last 11 years, handling all administrative and accounting matters at Forum Resources Network.

Our own strong friendship prompted me to seek Elizabeth's reflections on the power of friends at work. These are her words:

> Having the opportunity to work with a group of people who became friends was an amazing gift. The workplace was an environment of collaboration, respect, and hard work, but was always, and almost most importantly, downright fun.

Ten years later, and despite the fact that we have all moved on, many of these connections remain, and we have been there for one another through marriages, divorces, and even deaths of loved ones.

One knows that for that brief period, we had an extraordinary experience and that it was serendipity that brought this group of people together. You never forget the people with whom you shared the most amazing, ridiculous, stressful, and hilarious moments of your professional life.

Buying into the Mission

Through these powerful examples, I'm convinced that having a shared purpose is a powerful force for building enduring friendships. What is great about that for the workplace is that every business has such a shared purpose. It's called a "mission statement."

While the mission of your business may completely omit the notion of building a family or meaningful friendship, the mere fact that you have a mission that everyone buys into is an agent for creating those bonds.

Having all your employees buy into this shared purpose requires either involving them in creating this mission or finding people who already believe in your mission. Unfortunately, it also means that sometimes you might need to free up those who do not buy in.

Takeaway

A common sense of purpose is critical for building a successful team or business. Facing challenges together with a spirit of shared mission builds bonds that can take your company to the next level.

Entrepreneurs' Organization

Chapter

Creating Real
Friendships at Work

"Sometimes the hardest thing for us to do is trust enough to let someone help, especially when we've made ourselves vulnerable before and gotten burned."

Lilly Monroe, a "woman on the rise" and program participant in "Together We Bake," an Alexandria-based nonprofit that provides job training for women in need of a second chance

I hope by now you are ready to embark upon this journey to create real friendships at work. For some people that can be scary. Some CEOs have flat out told me that they have challenges with this concept. Their major concern has to do with how they can be friends with their employees and make the difficult decisions when needed.

To them I say two things:

Think about the impact of all the possible friendships in your company and not just about your own friendships. Friendships at work will happen whether or not you like it. Your role is to show your colleagues the way to have real friendships.

Real friendships, as we've discussed in this book, are not based on ignoring problems that arise, but instead are based on the ability to openly communicate the challenges. This is more easily done with a foundation of trust that is built on friendship.

I am truly thankful that I know of many enlightened companies in which the leaders value relationships as much as they do profit. That in itself will increase profit. Following are some ways to foster friendships at work.

Plan Company Off-sites and Retreats

Take your team on an off-site adventure. Many companies take their teams away for strategic planning and that is wonderful. In addition to strategic planning, a successful retreat will also focus on creating bonds, having open conversations, and having fun.

I've had the fortune to be a part of hundreds of these sessions, creating fond memories of meaningful connection, honest conversation, important strategic decisions and fun.

There are a few events that I remember not so fondly — those felt like a being in a marathon work session for 12 hours straight. Nobody gives his or her best, or is able to give his or her best, under those circumstances.

Successful off-sites start with pre-work through a survey, they have a clear agenda, they are inclusive of all participants and they are professionally facilitated to allow the participants to participate equally and effectively.

Helen Stefan Moreau, CEO of The Midtown Group in Washington, DC, has been committed to having these off-sites regularly, often in very nice establishments, as a way to express her gratitude for her amazing team. Everyone looks

119

forward to the retreats, not just as time to work on the business and the important relationships, but also as way to enjoy some pampering in beautiful places.

Feed the Village

Many of our clients bring in meals for the entire team. This provides an opportunity to break bread and to spend casual time with teammates.

By now we've all heard about Google providing meals around the clock. Not only does it increase efficiency and keep everyone around, but you can imagine the opportunities for people to interact and connect.

As noted earlier in this book, Jeff Marowits, partner at Keystone Strategy, has taken this even further by inviting clients and team-members to his home for dinner regularly. Think about how special that is in today's hectic lifestyle.

Participate in a Service Project

There are many causes all over the world or right in your neighborhood that can provide for an opportunity to give back. This will create a "feel good" opportunity for your team and another way for them to connect on a human level.

Sally Hurley, CEO of VIPdesk Connect in Alexandria, VA, and my better half, planned a day wherein all the employees pitched in for Together We Bake, an organization that trains women who have faced jail time to give them baking skills certification so they can find jobs.

Participate in a Sports League

Whether it's bowling or softball doesn't matter. What matters is that it's another way to engage your team members and have fun while making connections. An added bonus are the health benefits of doing something active.

When I was a senior at the University of Maryland, I worked at University College. Many of my colleagues from all levels of the organization played together in a softball league—a great way to deepen friendships.

Have a Family Day

A barbeque or a day at the beach can be a way to include family members to help create bonds and make it easier for some team members participate.

Provide a Game Room

Some are concerned that with this option, no one will get any work done. What I've noticed is that while some offices have pool tables, ping pong tables or dartboards, I don't see people playing throughout the day when they are working. But for those who want, it provides a break during lunch, plus an opportunity to have some fun and to connect with a teammate.

It's also been my observation that in those offices, the energy level is higher. You just feel it the moment you walk in. No one said you can't be productive and have fun!

Remember, too, that fun is one of the 7 Keys. Chris Johnson, CEO of Hollister Construction Services in Parsippany, NJ, has a "culture room." It's more like a culture center replete with three meeting rooms, a TV room with bean bags, a foosball table, a dartboard, a library and bar. Yes, a bar! I must say I've never seen anyone touch the alcohol, since they are indeed responsible adults and work comes first.

Provide a Workout Facility

Having healthy teammates goes a long way in having a healthy team culture. Exercise is proven to elevate your mood by the release of natural endorphins. Providing an easy way for your teammates to exercise not only promotes health but also provides for opportunities for everyone to connect and create friendships.

Consider Your Space

Think about your office layout. Is it siloed? Does the entire staff just sit in their offices with the door shut and no interaction? I can tell within a minute of visiting an office what kind of culture the organization has. If you want to foster interaction, the office layout and space for interaction is vital.

Tony Hsieh, CEO of Zappos, took this to another level by creating an entire campus in old town Las Vegas. As he puts it, you're more likely to have collisions with team-mates if you live, work, dine, shop and go to the dry cleaners within a few walkable blocks. By collisions he means potentially productive interactions with other Zappos employees.

Some companies now insist the meetings be face-to-face even if it means they

conduct the meeting by a video confer-
ence. The level of communication and
connection is much richer than just a
phone call and certainly an email or a
text.

Create Peer Groups & Peer Coaching Opportunities

A peer group is a small group of six to
eight people who have confidential
meetings to help each other grow. Lee
Wang, COO of WeddingWire, and Viraj
Gandhi of Paradyme Management, both
in Washington, DC, have created such
groups.

In an article in *Harvard Business Review*
about IBM, Jason Trujillo says, "A
manager can't have all the answers." As
such Jason and his team created a
marketplace platform called Coach.me

for coaching needs and solutions so employees can help one another.

Takeaway

The opportunities for creating con-nections are endless. Whether you take your team to a ballgame or a con-cert doesn't matter so much. What matters is that you create these oppor-tunities, and if you're the CEO you certainly shouldn't be the planner for any of them.

As the CEO your job is just to introduce the concept and set the budget and let your team run with it. If you are not the CEO, that shouldn't stop you from doing something!

Together We Bake

Chapter

Conclusion

"I want the companies and organizations that I am involved with to pursue a double-bottom line; be successful from a business standpoint but also be community-minded."

Ted Leonsis founder, chairman, majority owner and CEO of Monumental Sports & Entertainment, which owns and operates the Washington Capitals (NHL), Washington Wizards (NBA), Washington Mystics (WNBA) and Capital One Arena in downtown Washington, D.C.

By now I hope you're inspired. Inspired to create some new friendships; to rekindle an old friendship or one that has suffered; or, to uplift the culture of your company.

I hope you recognize that people show up not only to do their jobs but also to see their friends, to see people about whom they care deeply. Life is too short for a bunch of transactional relationships. To know that you truly care about me is one of the greatest feelings in the world, and to know that we share that mutual care is a treasured gift and a real friendship.

My observation in more than three decades of work in this very intimate space is that people hunger for authentic connection. To think that we can go to work day in and day out

without developing some real relationships is a fallacy.

Too many of us go through life not
realizing that our nextdoor neighbor or
our office mate is dealing with the same
challenges we are. We can choose to
keep those challenges from others out of
fear or as a matter of habit, or we can
choose to take a risk. I hope you'll
choose the latter.

In the process you'll discover who can be
trusted and who cannot, you'll find
support beyond what you've ever
imagined, and you'll make a few friends
along the way.

I wish each and every reader the fortune
to make the best of all 24 hours we get
every day. When you have real
relationships at work, the work— and
life itself—will ultimately be more
fulfilling, rewarding and productive.

Relationship Test

For each person you'd like to evaluate, consider how you think that person sees you and how you see that person on the seven categories. Please use a 10-point scale with 10 being best. What actions you will take to improve the relationship? Will you discuss with a friend?

Once you have evaluated one person, try another and another. After you have evaluated 10 relationships, you'll find some interesting information such as:

> Who may be a better friend than you thought?

> Who may be a worse friend than you thought?

133

What are the patterns that you display with all your friends in your perception and in their perception (once they've taken the test)?

What relationships may require a little effort for a big gain?

Take the test online at:
http://www.onlinefriendshiptest.com/

Who: _____	How I think I'm perceived	How I perceive this person
Judgment-Free		
Mischievous Fun		
Vulnerability		
Kind-truth		
Reliability		
Sharing & Generosity		
Shared Purpose & Values		
TOTAL		

About the Author

Mo Fathelbab is president and founder of Forum Resource, LLC (1997 to the present) and co-founder of Harvard Business School alumni forums. He is the  author of the best-selling book, *Forum: The Secret Advantage of Successful Leaders.*

Prior to forming his company, Mo served as executive director of Entrepreneurs' Organization (1991-1997), where he created the Forum program content and initiated hundreds of CEO Forums. Mo has worked with more than 20,000 CEOs and Entrepreneurs over the course of nearly three decades in 33 countries.

Mo regularly speaks to groups of CEOs and their C suite as well as to chapters of YPO(Young Presidents' Organization,

EO(Entrepreneurs' Organization), as well as various audiences of more than 500 attendees. He has a popular TEDx talk and has appeared on many TV shows and podcasts as well as in many newspapers.

Personally, Mo is dedicated to health and fitness. He loves skiing, sailing and stand up paddle boarding. He has completed three marathons, plus an Ironman. In 2018, he placed first in USA Yoga's Midwest regional championships for men over 50 and went on to compete at nationals.

Mo lives in Alexandria VA with his much better half Sally Hurley and their amazing son, Eli.

Made in the USA
Middletown, DE
12 September 2018